Stone Dead

and other adventure stories

Stone Dead

and other adventure stories

Stone Dead

by

Rob Childs

**NINE THIEVES
stone circle**

Near the hostel there is an
ancient stone circle called
the "Nine Thieves", although
only seven of the tall
standing stones are now left.
Legends tell that these were
once a band of robbers who
were turned to stone by witches!
If you look closely, you may
even be able to make out
weird "faces" scratched deep
into the stones...

Entry in a school hostel guidebook.

"Tick!" cried Paul. "You're on!"

Sarat shook his head. "Can't get me – I'm touching the stone."

"That's not fair, I ticked you first," Paul moaned. He went off to sulk on a small mound outside the entrance to the stone circle.

Alex flopped beside him.

"Come on, Paul, it's only a game."

"Oh, it's not that," he sighed. "Guess I'm just a bit sad we're all going home tomorrow. It's been a great week here."

"Sure has," agreed Sarat. "Thanks to Alex's rich dad paying for the whole class to stay at the hostel."

"I couldn't have come on this trip otherwise," Paul admitted. He gazed at the broken ring of crooked stones. "Bet this place looks dead spooky at night. Perhaps the witches even come out and dance around it and cast magic spells!"

"Rubbish!" Sarat scoffed. "You don't believe that stupid story in the guidebook, do you? There are no such things as witches."

Paul shrugged. "Well, there used to be. Anyway, what about those faces in the stones?"

"*Faces!* They're just a load of old scratch marks," Sarat laughed. "C'mon, let's run back to the hostel and find Tim. We've got to make sure everything's OK for our midnight feast."

The four boys shared two sets of bunk beds in their small dormitory and had been planning their farewell feast all week. Unknown to them, however, they were not the only ones making plans for late that night...

It was well into the early hours of the morning when Paul's dreams were disturbed by torchlight. Still groggy with sleep, he looked across the room to see two men pulling Alex out of the opposite lower bunk.

At first, Paul thought he must be having a nightmare. It was only after Alex cried out as they carried him through the door that Paul's brain clicked into gear and he realized what had actually happened.

He jumped out of bed. "Sarat! Tim! C'mon – wake up!" he yelled, shaking them roughly from their top bunks. "I think Alex has been kidnapped!"

Two minutes later, wearing trainers with coats pulled over their pyjamas, Paul and Sarat were darting into the wood next to the hostel.

"We shouldn't be doing this," Sarat hissed. "It isn't a good idea."

"Shut up and keep moving. Tim's gone to tell the teachers. We've got to follow those two kidnappers. If we wait, we'll lose them – and Alex."

Sarat was about to argue further when Paul cut him short. "Look! Torches – over there."

The boys slipped along a trackway towards the bobbing lights, quickly closing the gap. They knew they had to try and delay the men somehow and hold them up for a while until help arrived. Paul picked up a few loose stones and threw one over the kidnappers' heads. Another thudded into a tree trunk nearby.

Sarat joined in and a shower of small stones and sticks plopped into the undergrowth all around the kidnappers. They had not expected anyone to be on their trail so soon, and in the confusion Alex seized his chance. He leapt up at the man holding him, scratching his cheek and drawing blood. The kidnapper cursed in pain and surprise as Alex wriggled free and bolted away barefoot through the trees.

The other man started after him but
didn't get far. He ran straight into Paul's path
and was knocked to the ground by the full
force of a thick branch swung into his face.
Blood spurted from the man's nose.

"Let's get out of here fast!" cried Sarat in
panic. "Where's Alex?"

"He went that-a-way," Paul shouted
back, pointing. "After him!"

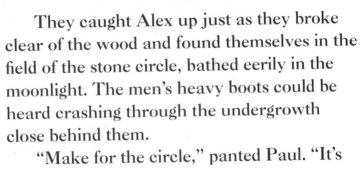

They caught Alex up just as they broke clear of the wood and found themselves in the field of the stone circle, bathed eerily in the moonlight. The men's heavy boots could be heard crashing through the undergrowth close behind them.

"Make for the circle," panted Paul. "It's our only chance."

It was the most terrifying game of hide-and-seek the boys had ever played. As they dodged among the long shadows cast by the seven stones, each of them was nearly grabbed by the kidnappers more than once. They managed to twist away from every angry, clumsy lunge just in time.

13

Then, for a fleeting second, all three boys were outside the circle and both men inside. In that instant the world seemed to change. Everybody stopped dead in fright, struck by a powerful blast of wind. The ground trembled and the moonlight went out, just like someone had thrown a giant switch.

"What's going on?" screamed Sarat.

Neither of his friends could answer. They were staring in horrified fascination at the scene inside the circle. The ancient stones were glowing in the darkness and the men were clawing desperately at the spaces between them. They stumbled from one to another, their faces wild with fear, calling out silently and hammering with their fists, as if at some invisible wall.

"They're trapped!" Alex whispered in shock. "They can't seem to get out..."

His voice trailed away. Without any signal, the boys turned on their heels and fled towards the hostel.

The following day, after a police search had found no trace of the kidnappers, all four boys plucked up the courage to return to the circle themselves for one last look.

"It just doesn't make sense," Sarat said, shaking his head. "Those men getting stuck inside there like that."

"And how did they escape before the police came?" asked Tim.

"Don't reckon they did," Paul said. "Have you lot counted the stones?"

"*Nine!*" gasped Alex, checking twice, hardly able to believe his eyes. "The Nine Thieves circle is full again!"

They peered closely at the two extra stones, both gnarled and scratched like the rest, and Paul exchanged a glance with **Alex**.

"Do you see what I see?" he asked.

Alex gulped and nodded. "Yes, I can see them."

Even Sarat had to admit that the "face" markings on the new stones did look strangely familiar.

"Just look at the bent nose on this ugly thing," Paul murmured, giving a little chuckle to himself.

Alex ran his finger down a long, damp groove in the other stone face and shuddered. "They threatened to kill me if Father didn't pay a ransom," he said quietly. "I'd recognize them again anywhere."

"*Anywhere?*" Paul stressed.

"Anywhere!" Alex repeated firmly and led the group back to the waiting coach, each lost in his own thoughts.

Bud and the Hunkpapas
by
Eileen Ramsay

Bud lay by the camp-fire and listened to the
settlers talking. He could tell from their voices
that they were very worried. Bud did not want
to be noticed and so he lay very still and quiet.

Sometimes he could pick out Colin's voice in all the talk. Colin McDonald was Bud's friend. He was ten years old, and had come west across America with his family, to live in the settlers' camp in that part of the Great Plains where the Hunkpapa tribe had their summer camps.

Colin was the only person in the settlers' camp who was willing to feed a stray dog like Bud. Bud couldn't round up cattle, and he was too friendly to be any use as a watch dog. Colin's father thought Bud was useless, and so Bud tried hard to keep out of his way. Now he lay still; only his ears showed that he was listening.

"I am sure that they are preparing to attack." That was Colin's father's voice.

"But they're our friends," Colin was saying. "Why should they attack us after all they did for us last winter?" The boy's voice broke a little – he was remembering how his mother and sister had died in the terrible snows that swept across the plains – and Bud wanted to go to him. He lay still. Later he would comfort Colin.

"They think one of us killed Red Cloud's son," said Mr McDonald. "The boy's coat is missing."

"Don't be stupid, McDonald. Why would anyone kill for a jacket?" That harsh voice belonged to Sam Glover. Bud kept well away from him too. At least Mr McDonald never kicked.

"It was a very special jacket," broke in old Mrs Robertson. "That embroidery would fetch quite a price in a store back East."

Then came Colin's voice again. "You're not saying that one of us killed Bear Cub, just for a beaded jacket?"

His young voice was so angry that again Bud wanted to go to him but he needed to keep well away from Colin's dad.

"Bear Cub was my friend," said Colin sadly.

Mr McDonald suddenly seemed to realize that his young son was still by the camp-fire. "Go to the wagon, Colin, and go to sleep," he said in an angry voice.

Colin got up and Bud slunk along beside him to the McDonalds' wagon. He hated to hear Colin sound so sad. He knew that Colin and the young Hunkpapa had been good friends. He also knew who had pushed young Bear Cub over the cliff after wounding him and stealing his beautiful jacket. There was no way that he could tell Colin though. Or was there?

"Isn't it awful, Bud?" said Colin as they lay side by side under the blanket on the floor of the wagon. "The Hunkpapas were so good to us when we got here from the East. They brought us meat and different berries and kept us alive last winter when we hadn't expected such dreadful weather. Father really wanted to stay here and to start building cabins by the river, and it looked as if Red Cloud was ready to share this plain with us. There's space for everyone; plenty of food in the summer, and we could have farmed and saved supplies for winter. We'd have shared with the Hunkpapas. We would all have been good friends, but now Bear Cub is dead and Red Cloud is on the warpath."

Bud pushed his cold nose against his young master in sympathy and Colin scratched him in that special place on his chest and they both fell asleep.

The next morning Bud and Colin were awakened very early by the sound of drums. Mr McDonald was already awake.

"We're pulling the wagons into a circle, Colin. The Hunkpapas will attack from every direction and a circle is the easiest way to guard the camp. Hitch up the horses and keep that useless mutt out from under my feet. I'd shoot him but I'll need every bullet I have before the day's out."

Bud knew the best thing was to keep well out of everyone's way. He waited until Colin was busy helping his father and the other men and boys, and then he raced out of the wagon train. He did what Bud and Colin always did when they had time for fun. He headed for Red Cloud's camp.

As usual the dog could smell the special scent of the Hunkpapa camp long before he got there. Instinct told him to stay hidden and to watch. The faces he saw were not the usual smiling happy ones. Today the Hunkpapas' faces were painted and they looked very fierce. Bud turned and ran as fast as he could back to his own camp.

Colin was happy to see him.
"I was afraid I'd never see you again, Bud," said Colin as he hugged the exhausted little dog. "There's going to be a big battle soon and there are hundreds of Red Cloud's men and only thirty-two of us, counting me. I'm not so scared, somehow, with you here."

"Get under the wagon, Colin, and stay there for now." Mr McDonald no longer sounded angry. He sounded sad as he handed his son a gun that had only been used for shooting hares. "You'll be with the men and the older boys when the shooting starts."

Bud lay for a while beside Colin. Yes, he could smell bear grease again. Somewhere in the camp there was bear grease – but it was the Hunkpapas, not the settlers, who used that. Silently Bud crept away, following that smell. It led him to another wagon, Sam Glover's wagon. Bud stayed alert and listened carefully to hear if the owner was there.

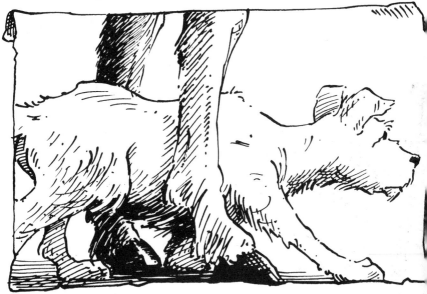

Silence. Sam Glover was talking with some of the other men on the far side of the camp. Bud jumped up on the wagon and crept under the canvas. He smelled bear grease strongly. But that was a Hunkpapa smell. It was the smell of young Bear Cub.

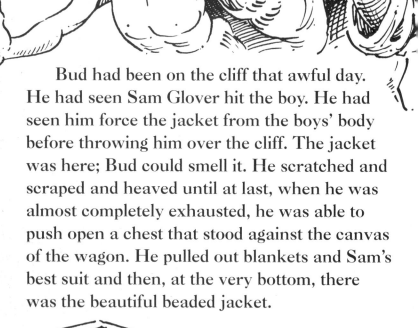

Bud had been on the cliff that awful day.
He had seen Sam Glover hit the boy. He had
seen him force the jacket from the boys' body
before throwing him over the cliff. The jacket
was here; Bud could smell it. He scratched and
scraped and heaved until at last, when he was
almost completely exhausted, he was able to
push open a chest that stood against the canvas
of the wagon. He pulled out blankets and Sam's
best suit and then, at the very bottom, there
was the beautiful beaded jacket.

Just as Bud grasped it in his strong jaws, Sam Glover returned to his wagon.

His gun was already in his hand.

Bud jumped from the wagon, followed by a gun shot.

Mr McDonald saw the little dog fall to the ground. The beaded jacket lay in the dust.

Now there were two splashes of blood on its lovely beading; the blood of the dog and the blood of the chief's son.

Mr McDonald realized what had happened. Quickly, he overpowered the angry Glover and put him under guard. Bravely, Colin's dad rode out of the circle of wagons and took the jacket to the Hunkpapa camp. Patiently and sadly, Red Cloud listened to the explanation.

We will punish Sam Glover according to our own laws, Red Cloud. We ask you not to punish all of us.

Red Cloud held the beaded jacket in his strong hands.

Your son was my son's friend. For the sake of all our sons, I will stop our drums.

Mr McDonald rode back to the wagons to tell the settlers that they were going to be able to stay. With him he brought some special medicine for Bud.

"When we build our cabin," said Mr McDonald, "there will be a place for a dog."

"You hear that, Bud?" asked Colin. "We're building a cabin and you are the official McDonald family dog."

Bud heard the happiness in Colin's voice. If Colin was happy, he was happy. He raised his head and yelped.

It's All in your Mind, Anna
by
David Clayton

Why do clocks zoom like rockets when you're on holiday and crawl like tortoises when you're waiting to do something good?

Maybe they don't. But that's the way I felt the day Suzie Strange invited me round to try her dad's new invention, FUTURE VISION.

I could almost hear myself bragging at school.

"You lot have just been playing ordinary computer games. I've had a go at FUTURE VISION!"

But, to tell you the truth, I didn't have a clue what it was myself.

Anyway, it happened like this. Suzie's dad is a boffin. He's a weirdo but brainy. So there are always new computer games to play at her house.

WOOP WOOP WOOP

WEIRDO

"This is different," she said.
"It's a sort of virtual reality thing."
"I've tried that," I scoffed.
"I only said 'sort of'," she sniffed. "This is new. This will blow your mind."

MIND BLOWING.

I just couldn't wait to have a go!

But, on the other hand, I was a bit puzzled. You see, I'd had a bit of an argument with Suzie the week before about some joke soap I slipped in her PE bag. Well, her face only stayed green for three days before the colour washed off. Anyway, Suzie was not happy with me.

But, there I was, walking in through Suzie's front door. And, there she was with her toothy grin and shiny blue eyes.

A voice in my head said "GET OUT OF HERE!" but I didn't pay any attention. I was too excited by the promise of Future Vision.

A clock ticked loudly as we crossed the hall, big as a football pitch. On we went, up the dark, steep stairs, and, all the time, Suzie smiled.

Great! Everything was OK between us again, I thought.

"The new game is in here," said Suzie, pushing open a door leading to a massive room with no windows.

Not only were there no windows, I couldn't see any computers either. Weird!

Now, that little voice inside me was calling louder than ever.

"GET OUT NOW WHILE YOU CAN!" it said.

"Shut up!" I snapped.

"I never said a word," said Suzie.

"Sorry, I didn't mean you," I said. "What do I do? There's nothing here!" I could hardly see anything in the greeny light.

"Yes, there is! Put this on."

She gave me a silver helmet. It was round as a goldfish bowl with with no window in it at all. Wires snaked everywhere but I still couldn't see any computer.

"DON'T DO IT!" shouted the voice.

But where was the harm in just playing a game?

I put the helmet on.

CLICK! LOCKED IN!

The room was blue now. Same size, same shape, same door, but Suzie was gone! I felt as if icy spiders were running over my skin.

"What now?" I asked.

"Now you're in our world,
Anna!" said a voice a little like
Suzie's but spooky.

"Your house, you mean?" I said.

"HA! HA! HA!" boomed the voice
mockingly. "No! OUR WORLD! Look at me!"

I turned. The creature behind me was two
metres tall, dressed in a glittery gold suit
covered in silver stars. But something about its
eyes made it look strangely like Suzie.

UH-OH! TROUBLE!

"Suzie? I'm sorry..." I started even though I
wasn't sure where she was.

The Suzie-like figure said nothing.

"I promise I won't..."

"The game is 'Space Hunter'!" the creature boomed. "You have one minute's start."

"I don't like this, Suzie. Can't we just play ordinary computer games?"

But the cold voice kept on. " ... and if we catch you..."

"WE?" I asked.

"YES!" many voices replied.

I looked around – and there were nine more of them! Nine more creatures with Suzie's shiny eyes!

One minute's start....

"Well?" I asked. "What *does* happen if you catch me? What happens if I won't play?"

ZAPPPPPPPPPP!!!!!!!

"YAAAAAAAAAAA!!!!!!!"

There was a flash and suddenly my bottom was stinging like mad.

"I'm not playing this stupid game!" I yelled, pulling hard at my helmet, but it would not move at all.

The creature in front had a laser gun bigger than a hair dryer. Things were getting serious. Space Invaders was never like this! The aliens never had real guns, did they? Everybody knew that.

ZAPPPPPPPPPPP!!!!!!!!!!

"YAAAAAAAAAAAAA!!!!!!!!!!"

By now my bottom was almost on fire.

"Those were levels one and two. There are twenty-five levels of pain," said one of the Suzie creatures. "You have fifty-five seconds left."

I was off! Down what still looked something like Suzie's stairs. If those were levels one and two, I'd be frazzled like a fly by the time they got to level ten.

No more rubber frogs in your soup, Suzie, I thought. No more jelly in your trainers. But it was too late to say sorry. If I didn't leg it while I could, Suzie's mum would be hoovering me up off the carpet soon.

My legs were flying, flying along a shiny yellow path. I was outside. Soon I found myself in a park. Freaky trees and bushes in all shades of red, purple and blue were reaching for me. Stinging me. Slithering and sliding at me like thin, glowing jellyfish.

"ERRRRRRRR!!! GET AWAY !!!" I shouted.

Then I realized what a dope I'd been.

The Suzie creatures would know where I was now.

Stupid!

Then I heard my hunters, crunching, stomping, crashing along close behind in the park.

I looked left and I could see them. I looked right and they were there too!

Horror! Nowhere to hide!

Go! Go! Go!

I was off like a bullet, out of the park and down a glittery path.

I didn't know how many lives I had in this game. I didn't know any "cheats" and I didn't want to find out the hard way that I only had one life.

The Suzie robots came closer and closer. Now they ran ten in line like shiny soldiers.

There were no turn-offs at all on this path, left or right. It was like running down a shimmering pipeline.

Go! Go! Go!

Suddenly, I saw that the pathway led into a tunnel.

Would I be trapped in there? Would more hunters cut me off from the other end?

No use thinking about it.

ZAPPPPP!!!!!!!!

A laser shot came close by.

I had no choice. I plunged into the gloom of the tunnel, ducking and dodging like a fox. Steps echoed behind me. Close behind me.

ZAPPPP!!!!!!!!!!!

"YAAAAA!!!!!!!!!!!!!!!!!"

Got me!

It was over. Surely they would really fry me with the next shot.

A moment later I was out of the tunnel. A ring of light like a golden porthole popped up in the wall to the right. I dived for it and rolled out into yellow, dazzling sunshine.

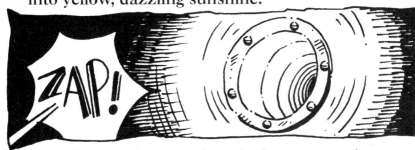

All around was a city of mirrors towering high into a golden sky. My legs were aching, my bottom burning, my head splitting. I came face to face with a mirror wall – and stopped.

There I was, two metres tall, in a red suit – and I had a laser too!

It was a different game now!

Two hunters found out
about this right away!

Around the corner they charged.
ZAPPPP! I hit them with my laser.
Down they went in a shower of sparks.
Eight to go!

Then I ran left into a maze, a zig-zag of
corners. Some walls were green, some were
black. Some were solid, some had spaces.

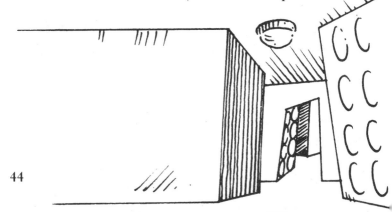

Were the rest of the hunters hiding there?

I tried a few corners.

Nothing!

Then WHAM! I ran right into a lone robot.

ZAPPPPP!!!!!!! I gave it level ten and BAM!
It shattered into hundreds of diamond stars.

DIAMONDS?

I picked one up, stuffed it into my pocket and
ran on.

Where now?

WHAT NOW?

I was going up and up and up a giant
stairway.

I knew this place. SUZIE'S HOUSE!

If, just if, I could get to the virtual reality
room without being caught, I could zap all
Professor Strange's virtual reality gear!

The game would be all over. I would
be FREE!

All I wanted was to be normal again. Not a fool or a show-off, just Suzie's friend. To say sorry for all the horrible tricks I played on her. Most of all, I wanted to get the nightmare helmet off and to go home!

But one step into the virtual reality room, I stopped.

Seven Suzie creatures stood in line.

Seven big zappers pointed at me.

This was IT! I closed my eyes.

Suddenly something was pulling at my helmet. Had another thing crept up behind me?

It really was all over for me!

"SUZIE!" Professor Strange's voice cut across the horror. Light dazzled my eyes as the helmet came off. And there stood Suzie's dad with his curly grey hair and gold glasses.

"You know I've told you NEVER to touch that program, or the Future Vision helmet!"

Suzie looked at her feet.

"Sorry," she mumbled.

"Me too!" I gasped, limping for the door as if I wasn't scared to death.

Suzie's dad saw me out.

"It was all in your mind, Anna!" he said. "You were quite safe, you know."

His eyes were as shiny and blue as metal as he spoke.

I gave him a hard stare but said nothing.

The door closed and I saw the bushes, brown, green and yellow, not red, purple and blue. I saw the tower blocks of the city – white, not shiny as mirrors.

I shook my head and wondered if it had been a dream.

But then something sharp dug into my leg. I put my hands into the pockets of my jeans and pulled out a glittering diamond star...

The Lamplighter
by
Alison Leonard

Maggie tried to get to sleep. She tossed and turned but she just couldn't drop off, so she went out on to the landing and called for Gran. Gran came straight away and gave her a hug. Maggie needed that hug, because she was miserable.

It was late at night. Maggie was sleeping at Gran's because her mother had been called down to the Emergency Centre at the factory where her father worked. What had happened? Some kind of accident. They didn't know what kind of accident, and they didn't know who might be hurt.

They sat together by the window. The street lamps were on, but the street was quiet and still. Maggie heard a car horn in the distance, and a dog barking in the house on the corner. A puddle glittered in the orange of the street lamps.

"I could tell you a story," said Gran. "A story that my gran told me when I was a girl your age."

"Oh?" said Maggie. She couldn't throw off the feeling of fear. For a fraction of a second she'd been curious about Gran's story, but then it washed over her again: Mum was down at the Emergency Centre, waiting to find out what happened to Dad.

"When will we know if he's all right?"

"I don't know," Gran answered. "We'll just have to wait."

Maggie cried, "I hate waiting! I can't wait!"

"My gran had to wait, too. Shall I tell you the story?"

Maggie couldn't listen. Story indeed! Gran always treated her as if she was a baby. But there was nothing else to do.

"All right," she said, sniffing. "Tell me."

"The story's called 'The Lamplighter', and it happened when my gran was about the same age as you. She was called Margaret.

"Margaret was a strange child. She believed in magic. She used to say magic spells and make magic potions. She collected spiders' webs from the corners of the bathroom, and dead leaves from flower pots, and colourings from tiny bottles in the kitchen cupboard, and she mixed them all in what she called her magic bowl. But nothing magic ever happened.

51

"One night, Margaret and her mother got some terrible news. It came by telegram. Margaret knew that a telegram would tell you one of two things: very, very good news, or very, very bad news. This was bad news. Her father, a sailor, had been in a terrible storm at sea, and he'd been tossed overboard. They didn't know whether he would be saved or drowned. Margaret and her mother just had to wait, and wait, and wait."

Maggie held her breath. Like we're waiting now, she thought.

"That night, Margaret couldn't sleep. She sat on the window ledge and looked out.

It was dusk outside in the street. She sat there long after her usual bed-time. The summer evenings were long like they are now, and it didn't get dark until late. One or two people were making their way home, and she could hear their feet in their hard wooden clogs going 'clop-clop-clop' on the cobbles.

"Then she heard a different step. It was almost like the step of a dancer. 'That'll be the lamplighter,' she thought. The lamplighter came along their street every evening. He was a tiny little man. He carried a long ladder that he balanced against the lamp-posts. He'd climb up the ladder with a lighted taper in his hand and light the gas in each lamp in turn.

"This particular night, Margaret was mixing a potion in her magic bowl with rose-petals, and bicarbonate of soda from the kitchen, and an actual dead spider that she'd found under her bed. She stirred it and stirred it, and said magic words over it. Then she waited for the magic to happen.

"The lamplighter came round the corner. His feet went 'tap-tap-tap', light as a dancer. He was singing a song, and the words of the song went like this:

There's Magic in the air tonight,
I feel it in my bones!
Go overground, go undergroun[d]
there's magic in the stones.

"Margaret was so surprised to hear him singing about magic that her hand slipped on the bowl, and it tipped out of the window and spilled the magic potion all over the lamplighter. The bowl shattered into tiny pieces on the pavement around him.

"The next thing she knew, she wasn't sitting on the bedroom window ledge. She was standing on the pavement. She was wearing the lamplighter's old coat and shoes, and had a lighted taper in one hand and the ladder in the other. The ladder wasn't heavy, she could carry it quite easily. The lamplighter had completely disappeared.

" 'Well!' thought Margaret. 'What am I going to do now?'

"That was an easy enough question to answer. She was wearing the lamplighter's coat and shoes and carrying his taper and ladder, so she'd have to do his work. She'd have to light the lamps.

"But this was a magic night. The lamps lit up as soon as she came near them. She seemed to be moving as fast as magic. One moment she was in one street, the next moment she was in the next. In no time at all,

she'd lit all the lamps in every street. Now
she was standing right in the middle of
the town.

"There stood the huge old mill where her
mum worked every day. It was dark and silent.
Margaret leaned the ladder up against the
windows and peered inside. The spinning
machines weren't running with their deafening
'clackety-clack! clackety-clack!' like they did
all day. They lay quite still. Not a single cotton
thread shot off the machines to wind itself
round and round the reels.

"Margaret thought, 'Mum and the other mill-girls would like an easy day tomorrow. I'll do some spinning for them.' She lifted her taper. On the instant the mill was filled with light. The machines started: 'Clackety-clack! Clackety-clack!' The thread shot off on to the reels, neat as any mill manager could wish.

"She lowered the taper, and the lights went out. Once again the machines lay silent and still.

"Margaret climbed down from the ladder. 'Where shall I go now?' she wondered. 'I know. Up on the moor.'

"As soon as she thought about it, the lamplighter's magic flew her up there. Ladder in one hand, lighted taper in the other, she flew through the air to the top of the moor.

"The moor lay in darkness. But, as she stood there, the moon came out from behind a cloud, and she could see the glimmer of heather and gorse. Down below her lay the silent town, the huge mills, the long rows of little houses climbing up the hillside. She imagined a girl lying wide-eyed in bed, tossing anxiously from side to side, not able to sleep. 'If I lift my lighted taper,' she thought, 'that girl will fall quietly asleep.' So she lifted her taper, and she knew it had happened.

"She put down the ladder and looked out over the town. Far away, farther than her eyes could make out, lay the sea. Farther away still lay the ocean, with its storms and tempests, where ships tossed and heaved and were toppled by vast waves.

"Margaret looked at the lamplighter's taper in her hand. 'If I lift it up,' she thought, 'will it bring my father safely home?' She couldn't answer the question, but she lifted it up all the same.

" 'Now,' she wondered, 'how am I going to get back?' As soon as she'd thought the thought, she found herself in the air, with the ladder in one hand and the magic taper in the other. Over mills and terraced houses she flew.

Next thing, she was sitting in her night-clothes on the window ledge.

"She looked out and saw the lamplighter, up on his ladder, lighting the lamp outside her house. He was singing:

There's magic in the air tonight,
I feel it in my bones!
Go overground, go underground,
there's magic in the stones.

"Then he climbed down the ladder, tucked it under his arm and went on his way. Just before he went round the corner, he looked back at the broken pieces of magic bowl that lay on the pavement. Then he looked up at Margaret and gave her a wave. She waved back, and the lamplighter disappeared.

61

"Suddenly, Margaret felt more tired than she'd ever felt in her life before. She got down from the window ledge, padded over to her bed, crawled under the covers and fell fast asleep."

Gran stopped speaking, and paused. Maggie looked up at her.

"Was her father saved, or was he drowned?"

"The magic didn't happen straight away," said Gran. "She didn't find out for a whole long week. There were no telephones then to give people news. But..."

"But?"

"One day, after Margaret – who was my gran, remember – came home from school, she was sitting eating her bread and jam at the kitchen table. Her mother was doing some washing up at the big pot sink. The back door opened, and there he stood."

"Her father," said Maggie.

"Yes," said Gran.

Maggie sighed a long sigh.

"Now, young lady," said Gran. "Let's get you back into bed."

Maggie lay and stared at her bedroom ceiling. In her mind's eye, she could see the sailor, standing smiling at the back kitchen door. Then she could see in her mind's eye her own father, standing in the kitchen downstairs.

Gran was just going out of the bedroom door. "Will Dad be all right?" Maggie asked her.

"I don't know," said Gran. "Sometimes magic works, and sometimes it doesn't."

"It's got to work," said Maggie. "It's got to work *now.*"

"We'll see," said Gran. "Go to sleep now."

And, like magic, Maggie went straight to sleep.